P9-DBI-394

painting china

painting china

Creative ideas for home ceramics

Mary Fellows
Photography by Michelle Garrett

southwater

738.15
FEL

This edition is published by Southwater

Distributed in the UK by
The Manning Partnership
251–253 London Road East
Batheaston
Bath BA1 7RL
UK
tel. (0044) 01225 852 727
fax (0044) 01225 852 852

Distributed in Australia by
Sandstone Publishing
Unit 1, 360 Norton Street
Leichhardt
New South Wales 2040
Australia
tel. (0061) 2 9560 7888
fax (0061) 2 9560 7488

Distributed in New Zealand by
Five Mile Press NZ
PO Box 33-1071
Takapuna
Auckland 9
New Zealand
tel. (0064) 9 4444 144
fax (0064) 9 4444 518

All rights reserved. No part of this publication may be reproduced, stored in a
retrieval system, or transmitted in any way or by any means, electronic,
mechanical, photocopying, recording or otherwise, without the prior written
permission of the copyright holder.

Southwater is an imprint of Anness Publishing Limited
© 1998, 2000 Anness Publishing Limited

1 3 5 7 9 10 8 6 4 2

Publisher: Joanna Lorenz
Editor: Sarah Ainley
Designer: Bobbie Colgate Stone
Step photographer: Rodney Forte
Illustrators: Madeleine David and Lucinda Ganderton

Previously published as *Inspirations: Decorating China*

CONTENTS

INTRODUCTION

Until very recently, to have individually designed china in your home usually meant paying a lot of money for hand-painted pieces from well known craftspeople. If you tried to recreate your own look the china was definitely for display purposes only unless you had access to a kiln. With the introduction of specialist china paints everything has changed: you can now paint on whatever you like and be sure that your designs will last.

All you need is plain china to work on although you could also add decoration to striped china. The colours you can use are endless: there is a huge selection available in the shops but you may even prefer to mix up colours of your own. Use the template designs at the back of the book, create freehand designs or stencil or stamp away to your heart's desire on anything from just one plate to an entire tea service.

In this book we show you a variety of designs decorating a range of china pieces, from plates to lampbases and tiles. Easy-to-follow step-by-step instructions are given for each of the 20 projects in the book, and a comprehensive techniques section covers all of the basic skills you will need to get started.

Once you have had a look through the book you will see for yourself how easy it is to paint your own china. Just have a go, and brighten up your breakfast table with some cheery tableware.

Deborah Barker

SNOWFLAKE PLATE

A set of delicately frosted plates would look terrific for winter dinner settings. You can make up as many differently designed snowflakes as you like to decorate the china.

YOU WILL NEED
plain china plate
cleaning fluid
cloth
pencil
drinking glass or beaker
masking film (frisket paper)
scissors
craft knife or scalpel
self-healing cutting mat
water-based ceramic paints: blue, white and gold
paint dish
sponge

1 Clean the plate. Draw round an upturned drinking glass or beaker on to the backing paper of masking film (frisket paper), to make about 8 circles.

2 Using a pair of scissors, cut out the circles.

3 Fold each circle in half.

4 Crease each semi-circle twice to make three equal sections. Fold these sections over each other to make a triangle with one curved edge.

5 Draw a partial snowflake design on to the triangle and shade the areas that will be cut away. Ensure that parts of the folded edges remain intact, or the snowflake will fall apart when opened up.

6 Carefully cut out the design, using a craft knife or scalpel and self-healing cutting mat. Discard the leftover scraps of masking film.

7 Very carefully open out the folded cut-out to reveal a snowflake. Make several individual snowflakes and arrange them on the plate.

8 When you are pleased with the arrangement, peel off the backing paper and position the masking film firmly in place, ensuring all the edges are stuck down firmly.

9 Mix an ice blue paint in a paint dish. Load a large sponge cube with the paint and dab the plate all over to sponge it quite evenly. Let dry.

10 Mix a darker blue paint in a paint dish. Load another sponge cube with paint and sponge around the inner and outer rim lightly. Add a little of this colour to each snowflake. Leave to dry.

11 Load a third sponge cube with gold paint and dab this lightly around the edge of the plate to pick it out. Pick out the inner rim and darker areas of the plate in the same way.

12 Before the paint is dry, remove the masking film cut-outs, using a scalpel if necessary. To make the plate foodsafe it should be fired in a kiln, according to the paint manufacturer's instructions.

HAND-PAINTED MUGS

A set of plain-glazed earthenware mugs can be made more interesting by adding some contrasting decoration. Where the set is made of different coloured mugs, use paints that match the original colours of other mugs to make the set more harmonious. Keep the decoration at least 3 cm / 1¼ in below the rim for safe use, unless you intend to fire the mugs in a pottery kiln.

YOU WILL NEED
4 plain colour-glazed earthenware mugs
cleaning fluid
cloth
pencils, one with eraser tip
water-based ceramic paints in contrasting
colours plus white
paint palette
artist's paintbrushes, one fine

1 Thoroughly clean the mugs. Pencil several differently sized circles all around one of the mugs, leaving the top 5 cm/2 in clear. Draw the circles freehand so that they are not perfectly formed.

2 Mix up your first contrast colour, adding some white to make it opaque.

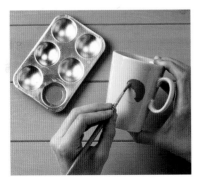

3 Fill in a circle on one of the mugs in a contrasting colour. Before the paint has dried, mark out a spiral pattern, as described in step 4.

4 Starting in the middle of the circle and using the eraser tip of a pencil, draw the spiral out to the edge. Try to do this in one movement for a neater design.

5 Paint in each remaining circle in turn, drawing out a spiral before the paint dries.

6 Using a fine paintbrush, paint radiating lines around the spirals. Leave to dry.

7 Using a fine paintbrush, paint a line detail down the outside of the handle.

8 Repeat the design on each mug, using contrasting colours, if liked.

Above: A set of mugs in different colours is given unity by matching and contrasting the painted design.

MOSAIC FLOWERPOT AND SAUCER

*Terracotta plant pots can be rather plain, but are easy to enliven with a bright interior
coating and an exterior checkerboard design printed in several cheerful colours.*

YOU WILL NEED
terracotta flowerpot and saucer
cleaning fluid
cloth
erasers
craft knife
pen
enamel paints: dark blue, green, yellow and lilac
paint palette
scrap paper
medium and large artist's paintbrushes

1 Thoroughly clean the flowerpot and saucer, using
cleaning fluid and a cloth. Cut the erasers into
long rectangular blocks. You will need one block for
each colour. Mark the same sized square on one end
of each eraser block and trim the ends to size.

2 Put a little of each colour into a paint palette,
and test print with each eraser block on scrap
paper until you are familiar with the technique.

3 When you are happy with the result, print
a square with the first colour on to the rim of
the flowerpot.

4 Using a second colour, print another square next to the first one, leaving a small gap between the two colours. Using a random sequence of colours, continue printing around the rim of the flowerpot to make two rows of squares. Leave to dry.

5 Print around the main body of the flowerpot in the same way as for the rim, starting at the top and leaving gaps between the squares. Continue to change the paint colour randomly and avoid creating diagonal runs or stripes of any one colour.

6 Gradually work down the flowerpot. The narrowing shape of the pot will mean that the squares have to be printed closer together as you work downwards, with narrow gaps of terracotta showing through near the base. Leave to dry.

7 Meanwhile, using a medium paintbrush, paint the upper face of the saucer with one of the colours used for the pot. Don't paint the rim. Let dry.

8 Finally, use a large paintbrush to paint inside the pot with a different colour from that used for the saucer. Let the paint dry completely.

CARNIVAL VASE

This wildly painted vase is a celebration in itself. The colours and patterns used here are merely suggestions. You can use the ideas to create your own joyful sequence of colours and shapes.

YOU WILL NEED
plain white vase
cleaning fluid
cloth
felt-tipped pen or soft pencil
enamel paints: pale green, dark green,
red, orange and black
artist's paintbrushes, one very fine
paint palette
tissue

1 Clean the vase. Draw irregular bands horizontally around the vase, dividing it into eight. Do this quite freely, using a felt-tipped pen or soft pencil.

2 Divide three of the bands vertically into an even number of sections. The bands do not need to be completely regular.

3 Select a sectioned band, here the middle one, and draw a rolling wave in each section of that band round the vase. Draw the waves freehand but make sure they flow into one another.

4 In a second sectioned band, here the lowest one, draw vertical zigzags to divide the sections into triangles. Then divide another band into small squares, here a double row below the triangles, ensuring that there is an even number of squares around the vase.

5 Fill another band with hand-drawn circles, some of them nudging the edges of the band.

6 Paint alternate squares of the double row pale green. Then paint the band around the small circles pale green as well. Leave to dry before painting the next section.

7 Paint alternate sections of a third sectioned horizontal band, here the one around the neck of the vase, dark green. Paint the downward pointing triangles dark green, too. Leave to dry. ▶

8 Paint the small circles red, leaving a small band of original vase showing through between the red and the surrounding pale green. Then paint the wave red. Leave to dry.

9 Paint the three remaining plain bands, including around the neck, in orange, leaving some of the white showing through if desired. Paint inside the neck, too. Leave to dry.

10 When the paint is completely dry, wipe off any pen marks using a damp tissue.

11 Using a very fine paintbrush, paint outlines to emphasize colour transitions. Make the lines quite free, allowing them to go over the edges of the colours. Leave to dry.

AUTUMN LEAF COFFEE POT

The application of a few gold blocks of colour, highlighted by sketched leaf outlines,
positioned like falling leaves, quickly turns a plain white coffee pot into
an elegant piece of pottery.

YOU WILL NEED
pencils, hard and soft
stencil card (cardboard)
craft knife or scalpel
metal ruler
self-healing cutting mat
carbon paper
fine felt-tipped pen
plain coffee pot
cleaning fluid
cloth
masking tape
sponge
water-based ceramic paints: gold and black
paint dish
fine artist's paintbrush

1 Use a hard pencil to draw an irregular four-sided shape, approximately 2 cm/¾ in square, on to a piece of stencil card (cardboard).

2 Using a sharp craft knife or scalpel, a metal ruler and self-healing cutting mat, cut the shape away, leaving the card border intact.

3 Place the stencil over a piece of carbon paper, carbon side down. Very gently draw the outline of a leaf with centre vein through the stencil hole on to the carbon paper, using a fine felt-tipped pen.

4 Thoroughly clean the coffee pot, using cleaning fluid and a cloth. Attach the stencil to the pot using masking tape.

5 Load a small cube of sponge with gold paint and lightly dab it over the stencil, taking care not to go over the outside edge of the card. Leave to dry.

6 Once the paint is completely dry, remove the stencil.

7 Replace the stencil in a new position, rotating it slightly. Avoid sticking the tape over the previously painted shape. Dab the stencil with gold paint as before. Repeat steps 5–7 to create a random pattern over the entire pot, including the spout and lid.

8 Using masking tape, carefully attach the carbon paper with the leaf drawing over a stencilled gold shape so that the leaf outline overlaps the edge of colour. With a sharp soft pencil, very lightly trace the leaf shape on to the pot.

9 Remove the carbon paper and trace the shape over the remaining blocks of gold colour as described in step 8. Position the stencils at slightly different angles each time.

10 Darken the leaf outlines with black paint, using a fine paintbrush. Leave to dry.

11 Fill in the leaf veins with black paint. Leave the paint to dry.

12 Finish off the design by painting the knob of the coffee pot lid with gold paint. Let dry.

PASTA BOWLS

The painted images in this design are applied to the bowls in a way that leaves them interestingly textured. The exact colour mixes used have been listed below, but you could vary the colours according to the paints you have available.

YOU WILL NEED
plain white pasta bowls
cleaning fluid
cloth
acrylic paints: mid blue, dark blue,
deep violet, green, white,
red and yellow
artist's paintbrushes
paint palette
tracing paper
soft pencil
drafting film (acetate)
matt acrylic varnish

1 Clean the bowls with the cleaning fluid and a cloth. Paint a rough background on the outside of the bowls, using water to weaken the consistency of the paint. A mix of mid and dark blue, deep violet, green, and white is used here. Leave to dry.

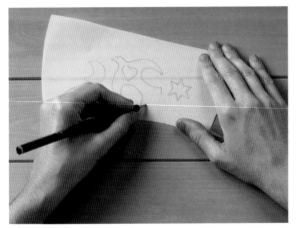

2 Draw a freehand dove image on to tracing paper and enlarge if necessary. Transfer the image on to drafting film (acetate). Do the same with any other images you are including.

3 On the other side of the drafting film, paint half of the dove image in white.

4 Before the paint dries, quickly press the shape on to the bowl. Peel off the drafting film and wipe it clean. When the image on the bowl is dry (this can be speeded up by using a hairdryer), paint the other half of the dove image in white and firmly press the shape on to the bowl again.

5 The texture of the dove outline will probably be very rough. Tidy it up using the mid blue and white paint until you get a shape you like.

6 When the painted dove image is dry, print the star shape using the same method as for the dove. Here the paint mix used is white, yellow and red.

7 Repeat the procedure to print the moon shape, using the yellow paint.

8 Paint the heart shape in the centre of the dove on the drafting film and transfer it to the bowl in the same way as above. Use a mix of yellow, red, and white. Leave to dry.

9 Tidy up the shape using the mixed paint colours until you are happy with the result. Leave to dry.

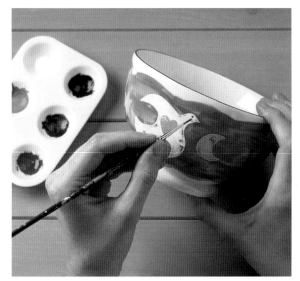

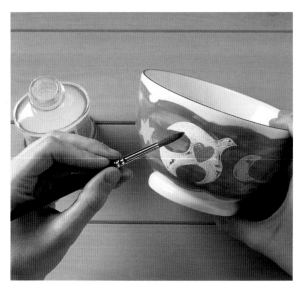

10 Paint in the dove's eye, using dark blue paint.

11 When all the paint is thoroughly dry, varnish the image area with matt acrylic varnish.

FUNKY CONDIMENT SET

This design works best with a salt and pepper set that is shaped with six flat sides. If your pots are not multi-faceted, simply divide them into six sections lengthways using a pencil: divide them first into two halves, then each half into three equal sections. The pots can be painted alike or with a slight variation, as here, to add interest.

YOU WILL NEED
plain salt and pepper pots (shakers)
cleaning fluid
cloth
soft pencil
masking fluid
artist's paintbrush
paint palette
water-based ceramic paints: turquoise,
dark pink and white
scalpel or compass

1 Thoroughly clean the pots, using cleaning fluid and a cloth. Draw small oval shapes on alternate sections of one of the pots (shakers).

2 Fill each oval with masking fluid. This needs to be quite thick, so it is best to apply two coats, allowing the first to dry before applying the second.

3 Apply circles of masking fluid around the holes in the top of one of the pots. Leave the masking fluid to dry completely.

31

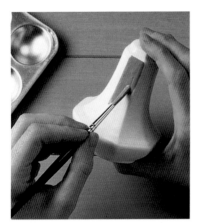

4 Apply the first colour of paint over the alternate sections marked with the oval shapes: here turquoise has been used. Use single strokes, taking care not to pull off the masking fluid.

5 Paint the base of the pot in a contrasting colour: here a dark pink has been used.

6 Next, lighten the colour used for the base with a little white paint and paint the top of the pot. Let dry.

7 Paint the bottom rim of each pot with the same light pink as for the top. Leave the paint to dry.

8 Using a scalpel or compass point, pierce the masking fluid in the centre of each oval shape and carefully peel it away. Repeat steps 2–8 for the second pot, or paint a variation design if you prefer.

SEASHORE BATHROOM SET

Imaginative designs applied to a plain soapdish and toothbrush holder will transform the look of your bathroom. Use this delightful watery motif with any combination of colours.

YOU WILL NEED
plain china soapdish and toothbrush holder or mug
cleaning fluid & cloth
tracing paper
soft pencil
plain paper
adhesive spray
carbon paper
scalpel or scissors
clear adhesive tape
felt-tipped pen
water-based ceramic paints: mid blue, ivory, turquoise, lemon, pink and dark blue
medium and fine artist's paintbrushes
paint palette

1 Thoroughly clean the china, using cleaning fluid and a cloth, to remove all traces of dust and dirt.

2 Trace the templates at the back of the book and enlarge if necessary. Transfer the designs on to a piece of plain paper. Spray the back of the paper with glue and stick on to a sheet of carbon paper, carbon side down. Cut out the designs, leaving a margin all round. Tape the designs on to the china pieces. Transfer the outlines lightly with a felt-tipped pen and remove the carbon paper designs.

3 Using a medium paintbrush, paint in the blue background colour on the soapdish and toothbrush holder. When completely dry, paint in the fish and shells on the soapdish.

4 Paint the fish and shells on the toothbrush holder in the same way as for the soapdish, using a medium paintbrush. Allow the paint to dry.

5 Using a fine paintbrush and dark blue paint, sketch in detailing for the fish and shells.

6 Add the border to the soap dish and the final touches to the toothbrush holder. Paint white dots and squiggles, to create a watery feel. Let dry.

STARBURST BATHROOM TILES

Plain white tiles can be painted with individual designs of your choice for a fraction of the price you would have to pay for shop-bought ones.

YOU WILL NEED
plain white tiles
cleaning fluid
cloth
tracing paper
soft pencil
acrylic paints: white, royal blue,
light blue, deep violet, burnt umber,
yellow and red
paint palette
artist's paintbrushes
drafting film (acetate)
paper towels
matt acrylic vanish

1 Thoroughly clean the tiles. Trace a rectangle on to the middle of a tile as a background shape.

2 Roughly paint the background shape in dark blue. The paint mix used here is white, royal blue, light blue, deep violet and burnt umber. Allow the paint to dry, using a hairdryer to speed up the process, if liked.

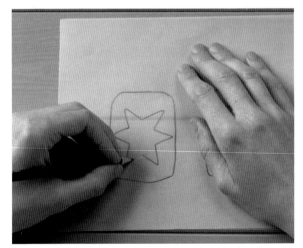

3 Use a soft pencil to draw a freehand star shape inside the rectangle on the tracing paper, and then transfer the star to the drafting film (acetate).

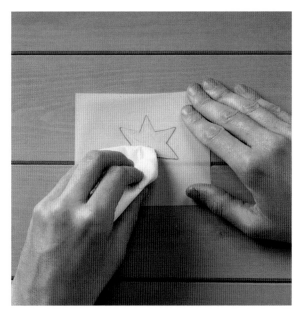

4 On the other side of the drafting film, paint the star in yellow, using a mix of the white, yellow and red paints.

5 Tidy up the star with a damp paper towel and touch up with the mixed paint until you are happy with the shape.

6 Before the paint dries, press the star lightly on to the background. Peel the film off and wipe it clean if you wish to reuse it. Let the paint dry.

7 When you have printed the star, check you are happy with the shape on the tile.

8 If the star did not print well the first time, touch up the shape with the mixed paint. Allow the paint to dry.

9 When the paint is completely dry, varnish over the painted area with matt acrylic varnish and leave to dry.

VEGETABLE STORAGE JARS

Storage jars are always useful, and when adorned with bold designs such as these colourful vegetables they add to the visual appeal of your kitchen. Alternatively, you can decorate them to give away as presents.

YOU WILL NEED
tracing paper
soft pencil
plain paper
adhesive spray
carbon paper
scalpel or scissors
plain china storage jars
cleaning fluid
cloth
clear adhesive tape
felt-tipped pen
water-based enamel paints: turquoise,
coral, ivory, blue and yellow
medium and fine artist's paintbrushes
paint palette

1 Trace the templates at the back of the book and enlarge if necessary. Transfer the designs on to a piece of paper. Spray the back of the paper with glue and stick it on to a sheet of carbon paper, carbon side down. Cut out the designs with a margin all round.

2 Clean the jars, using cleaning fluid and a cloth. Tape some of the designs on to one of the jars. Go over the outlines lightly with a felt-tipped pen to transfer the designs to the jar. Remove the carbon paper designs and repeat for the other jars.

3 Using a medium paintbrush, paint in the turquoise background colour on the jars and lids. Allow the paint to dry completely – this may take several days.

4 Mix up some red paint from the coral and ivory and paint in the chillis. Mix blue and yellow and paint the green of the vegetable leaves. Let dry.

5 Using a fine paintbrush and blue paint, sketch in detailing for the vegetables.

6 Paint the jar rims yellow and add small dots, using the ivory paint, for decoration. Let the paint dry completely.

Above: These brightly painted jars will become a focal point in any kitchen.

BEDROOM LAMPBASE

To paint a china lampbase, you will first need to dismantle it. This is a straightforward procedure but if you are in any doubt about rewiring the lamp, ask an electrician to do it for you.

YOU WILL NEED
ceramic lampbase
white spirit or cleaning fluid
cloth
soft pencil
tracing paper
plain paper
scissors or scalpel
carbon paper
clear adhesive tape
oil-based ceramic paints: lilac,
turquoise, pink, lime and black
medium and fine artist's paintbrushes
lampshade

1 Clean the lampbase, using white spirit or cleaning fluid and a cloth. Remove the electrics.

2 Trace the background template from the back of the book on to tracing paper and transfer to a piece of plain paper. Using the paper as a guide, transfer the background design on to the lampbase with a soft pencil.

3 Trace the pattern templates at the back of the book on to tracing paper. Copy the pattern designs from the tracing paper on to a sheet of plain paper. Cut out the designs with a pair of scissors or a scalpel, then attach the designs to carbon paper, using the clear adhesive tape.

4 Continue to trace and copy the designs, attaching them to pieces of carbon paper.

5 Paint the background of the lampbase, using a medium paintbrush. First paint in the lilac sections, then add the turquoise, pink and lime. Leave to dry.

6 To transfer the designs, first arrange them around the painted lampbase and then fix them in place, using the clear adhesive tape.

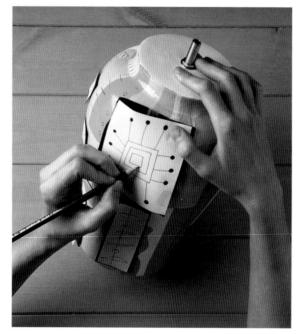

7 Use a soft pencil to transfer the design through the carbon paper on to the lampbase. Press light-ly on the plain paper to leave a clear print, holding the lampbase steady with your other hand.

8 Using black paint and a fine paintbrush, trace around the outline made by the carbon paper. When the paint is completely dry, attach the shade to the lampbase and refit the electrics.

SUMMER TEA SERVICE

Plain white china tea sets are often sold much cheaper than ready decorated ones. If the purity of an all white set does not appeal, you can customize it, transforming it into a desirable hand-painted collection. Try these specially-mixed colours, or your own combinations.

YOU WILL NEED
plain china tea cup, saucer and teapot
cleaning fluid & cloth
tracing paper
pencil
plain paper
spray adhesive
carbon paper & scissors
clear adhesive tape
felt-tipped pen
water-based enamel paints: lime, light green, pale lilac, pink and dark blue
paint palette
thick, medium and very fine artist's paintbrushes

1 Thoroughly clean the china, using cleaning fluid and a cloth to remove all traces of dust and dirt.

2 Trace the templates at the back of the book, enlarging them if necessary, and transfer them on to a piece of plain paper. Coat the back of the paper with spray adhesive and place this on top of a sheet of carbon paper, with the carbon side down. Cut out the uneven row of squares for the teapot, leaving a narrow margin.

3 Wrap the cut-out row of squares around the teapot, holding it in position with adhesive tape. Go over the drawn outline of the squares with a felt-tipped pen to transfer the outlines on to the teapot. Remove the carbon paper cut-outs.

4 Cut out the designs for the teacup and saucer. As before, using adhesive tape to hold the cut-outs in position on the china, trace over the design with a felt-tipped pen to transfer. Remove the carbon paper cut-outs.

5 Paint the background pastel colours on to the teapot, lid and saucer. The colours used here are lime and a light green. Allow the paint to dry completely.

6 Paint the background colour on to the teacup. Here the colour is a pale lilac. Allow the paint to dry thoroughly.

7 Fill the squares on the teacup with colour. Here they are being painted lime, green and pink. Leave the paint to dry.

8 Cut squares around the leaf and spiral designs. Tape some of these over the coloured squares around the cup and go over the designs with a felt-tipped pen to transfer the designs. Fill in the squares and transfer leaf and spiral designs to the teapot and saucer in the same way. Remove the cut-outs.

9 Using a very fine paintbrush, paint over the leaf and spiral designs on the teapot, cup and saucer in dark blue paint. Let dry. If you intend to use the tea service, it should first be fired in a pottery kiln according to the paint manufacturer's instructions.

CHILD'S TEASET

Imagine the delight this specially painted tea set featuring playful rabbits will bring to a child you know. This is just the sort of special gift that could be treasured for many a year.

YOU WILL NEED
plain china mug, bowl and plate
cleaning fluid & cloth
tracing paper
pencil
plain paper
adhesive spray
carbon paper
scissors
clear adhesive tape
felt-tipped pen
cotton bud (swab)
water-based enamel paints: yellow,
turquoise, red, green and blue
artist's paintbrushes, one fine

1 Thoroughly clean the mug, plate and bowl with cleaning fluid and a cloth.

2 Trace the templates for the rabbits and flower at the back of the book and transfer to a piece of plain paper. Spray the back of the paper with glue and place it on top of a sheet of carbon paper, with the carbon side down. Cut out around the drawings, leaving a narrow margin.

3 Arrange the cut-out drawings around the china pieces, holding them in place with clear adhesive tape. Go over the design with a felt-tipped pen to transfer the design to the surface of the china. Remove the cut-outs and clean up any smudges with a cotton bud (swab).

4 Paint the background areas of the centre of the bowl in yellow.

5 Paint the remaining background areas, here around the rim of the bowl, in turquoise.

6 Once the background paint is dry, start painting in the detail. Here the flowers are painted red, turquoise and green.

7 Using a fine paintbrush, paint over the outlines of the large rabbits and flowers in blue paint.

8 Paint over the outlines of the smaller rabbits on the rim of the plate, using the blue paint.

9 Finally, paint the handle of the mug turquoise. Let dry. The pieces should be fired in a pottery kiln in order to make them foodsafe.

1950s JUG AND BUTTER DISH

The fresh checkerboard scheme shown here is typical of the kitsch designs popular in the 1950s.
The style can be extended to other white ceramics to create an entire tableware set.

YOU WILL NEED
plain china jug (pitcher) and butter dish
white spirit or cleaning fluid & cloth
felt-tipped pen
ruler
coloured masking film (frisket paper)
scissors
tape measure
tracing paper
soft pencil
sponge
water-based ceramic paints: yellow,
blue, red and white
paint palette
fine artist's paintbrush

1 Clean the jug (pitcher) and butter dish, using white spirit or cleaning fluid and a cloth.

2 Mark 1 cm/½ in squares on the paper backing of the masking film (frisket paper) and cut out. Peel away the backing from each square and stick each one 1 cm/½ in apart along the top edge of the jug and butter dish. Use a tape measure for guidance. Stick a second row of squares beneath the first to form a checkerboard pattern. Repeat to make three rows on the jug and four on the dish.

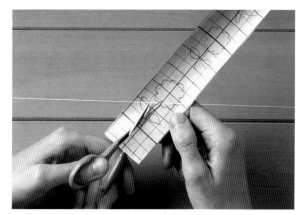

3 Draw a freehand rose on to tracing paper and enlarge if necessary. Transfer the rose to the paper backing of the masking film and cut out, using scissors. Make four rose cut-outs for the butter dish and two for the jug.

4 Peel away the paper backing and stick one rose lengthways to the centre of each side of the butter dish and one on either side of the jug.

5 Cut a 2 cm/¾ in wide strip of masking film the same length as the rim of the dish, and cut another one to the rim of the jug. Peel away the backing paper and stick the film along the bottom edge of the bottom row of squares.

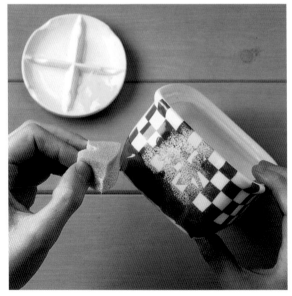

6 Cut a 1.5 cm/⅝ in cube of sponge. Load the sponge cube with yellow paint and apply the paint all over the checkerboard pattern. Leave to dry.

7 Carefully peel the masking film shapes off the jug and butter dish to reveal the pattern beneath.

▶

55

8 Mix some blue paint into the yellow to make a green. In the blank spaces left by the rose templates, paint in the stems and leaves freehand. Leave the paint to dry.

9 Mix up a darker green colour, and use this to paint details on to the stems and leaves. Leave to dry.

10 Mix up two shades of pink, using red and white paint. Paint the flowerhead area with the paler shade of pink and leave to dry. Add details for the petals with the darker shade of pink. Cut a piece of masking film 3 mm/⅛ in wide by 6 cm/2½ in long and wrap it around the base of the knob of the butter dish lid. Load a sponge with yellow paint and dab the knob all over to cover it in paint. Let dry.

ESPRESSO CUPS AND SAUCERS

The bright yellow stars on this coffee cup and saucer set shine out from the strong background,
making this a stunning design. A complete set would be a glorious addition to the dinner table.

YOU WILL NEED
4 plain espresso cups and saucers
white spirit or cleaning fluid
cloth
pen
coloured masking film (frisket paper)
scissors
sponge
water-based enamel paints: mid blue,
darker blue and yellow
paper towels
fine artist's paintbrush
cotton buds (swabs)

1 Thoroughly clean the china pieces with white spirit or cleaning fluid and a cloth.

2 Draw several star shapes on to masking film (frisket paper). Cut out the stars with scissors.

3 Remove the backing paper from the stars and stick them on to the first cup and saucer in a pleasing pattern.

4 Load a sponge cube with mid blue paint and dab the china all over with it. Leave the paint to dry completely.

5 Load another sponge cube with a darker shade of blue and lightly sponge over the light blue. Leave to dry.

6 Peel off the plastic stars and clean away any paint that has leaked beneath them, using a damp paper towel.

7 Using a fine paintbrush, fill in the stars with yellow paint. Use cotton buds (swabs) to neaten up the design, if necessary.

8 Clean up the rims of the cup and saucer, removing any excess paint. If you would like to use the cups and saucers, fire them first in a pottery kiln following the paint manufacturer's instructions.

CHECKERBOARD DINNER PLATE

Like so many successful designs, this stunning dinner plate owes its impact to its simplicity.
A table set with several of these plates would look just wonderful. You can create a set
in a matter of minutes.

YOU WILL NEED
plain white china plate
cleaning fluid
cloth
sponge
craft knife or scalpel
water-based enamel paints: blue,
green and yellow
paper towel
masking fluid
artist's paintbrushes
cotton buds (swabs)

1 Clean the plate. Cut several cubes of sponge for sponging the paint on to the plate. Holding the sponge taut as you slice a square down into the sponge will make cutting easy and the lines straight. Load the first sponge cube with blue paint and dab the plate to make a checkerboard pattern. Let dry.

2 Load a second sponge with green paint and dab it in the gaps between the blue squares.

3 Use a damp paper towel to wipe off any excess paint on the rim of the plate.

4 Paint a decorative border design around the rim of the plate with masking fluid and leave to dry.

5 Sponge blue paint all over the rim of the plate, leaving a narrow border around the central squares. Leave until the paint is dry.

6 Gently rub off the dried masking fluid with a damp paper towel to reveal the painted design.

7 Use yellow paint to highlight the design around the border, tidying up the design with cotton buds (swabs), if necessary. The plate should be fired in a pottery kiln before use.

ABSTRACT EGG CUPS

Wake up breakfast with individually designed egg cups. Styled as a set, no two designs will match exactly, giving each piece a unique pattern. The strong geometric theme shown here can be altered to create different looks.

YOU WILL NEED
2 plain egg cups
white spirit or cleaning fluid
cloth
pen
ruler
coloured masking film (frisket paper)
scissors or craft knife
sponge
water-based ceramic paints: black,
orange and blue
paint palette
black ceramic paint dot-and-line dispenser

1 Thoroughly clean the surface of the egg cups, using white spirit or cleaning fluid and a cloth.

2 On the paper side of the masking film (frisket paper), mark 3 mm/⅛ in wide strips the length of an egg cup. Cut out, remove the paper backing and stick the strips around each egg cup at random intervals lengthways. Mark and cut out four small circles and stick two on each egg cup, one above the other between two strips.

3 Cut three small cubes of sponge. Load one cube with black paint and dab it over the segment with the plastic circles to fill in completely between the strips. Leave to dry.

▶

4 Remove the plastic circles. Using the dot-and-line dispenser, mark in the details. Here, the edge of a circle is being partially filled in to create a single star effect.

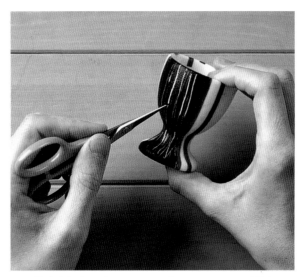

5 Dab black paint over another segment to fill it completely, then leave it until the paint is nearly dry. Using either the point of a closed pair of scissors or a craft knife, scratch lines in the paint to reveal the surface beneath.

6 Load a second sponge cube with orange paint and fill in two more segments. Leave to dry, then mark out rows of dots, using the paint dot-and-line dispenser.

7 Load the third sponge cube with blue paint and fill in another segment. Leave to dry. Peel away the masking film strips and clean away any excess paint with a craft knife. Using the dot-and-line dispenser, mark out zigzag patterns, as shown.

SUNFLOWER VASE

Sunflowers seem to be perennially popular. They make a wonderfully cheerful decorative motif for brightening up an otherwise plain vase.

YOU WILL NEED
plain white vase
cleaning fluid
cloth
tracing paper
soft pencil
masking tape
chinagraph pencils: yellow and blue
water-based enamel paints: yellow, pale green,
light brown, dark green, very pale brown and sky blue
paint palette
medium and fine artist's paintbrushes

1 Thoroughly clean the vase. Draw a freehand sun-flower design on to tracing paper and enlarge if necessary. Fix the tracing to the vase, using masking tape, and rub with a soft pencil to transfer the image.

2 Transfer the design all around the vase. Highlight each design with a yellow chinagraph pencil.

3 Fill in the petals with yellow paint and the stalks and leaves with pale green. Let dry.

4 Paint the flowerhead middles light brown. Include a circle of short lines around the edge of each flower centre. Let the paint dry.

5 Add detail to the leaves using a darker shade of green. Add dabs of very pale brown to the centre of each flowerhead middle. Let dry.

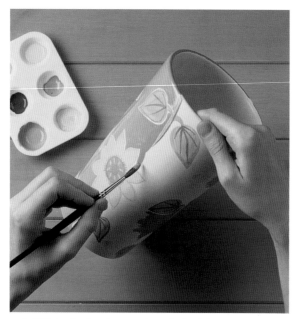

6 Fill in the background with sky blue, leaving a white edge showing around the flower. Let dry.

7 Finally, draw around the outline and middle detail of each flower with a blue chinagraph pencil.

KITCHEN HERB JARS

Herbs are best stored in the dark: plain china jars can be prettily decorated and displayed in the kitchen. Each of these jars bears a coloured lozenge which can be used, if done before the paint dries, to write the name of the herb contained within.

YOU WILL NEED
6 plain china herb jars
tracing paper
soft pencil
carbon paper
masking tape
cleaning fluid
cloth
blue chinagraph pencil
water-based enamel paints: blue,
lime green, dark green and turquoise
paint palette
artist's paintbrush
dried out felt-tipped pen

1 Draw a larger and a smaller leaf design on to two pieces of tracing paper, enlarging the designs if necessary. Attach the tracing paper to carbon paper, carbon side down, with masking tape.

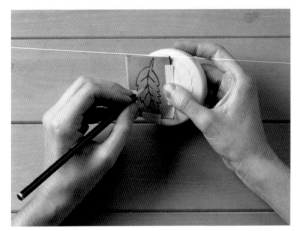

2 Clean the jars. Attach the tracing of the larger leaf on to the lid of a jar, to one side, and trace the outline with a pencil to transfer. Replace the tracing in another position on the lid and repeat.

3 Attach the smaller tracing to the side of a jar and trace the leaf outline on to the jar. Transfer the leaf outline several times in different places around the jar, leaving a large space in the centre of one side.

4 Using a blue chinagraph pencil, draw a freehand oval in the space you have left.

5 Fill in the oval with blue paint.

6 Before the paint dries, draw a design, pattern or a word, using an old dried out felt-tipped pen. The felt tip will remove the blue paint to reveal the white china beneath.

7 Paint the herb leaves lime green. Allow the paint to dry completely.

8 Add detail to the leaves in a darker green paint. Let dry.

9 Fill in the background in turquoise, leaving a thin white outline around each image.

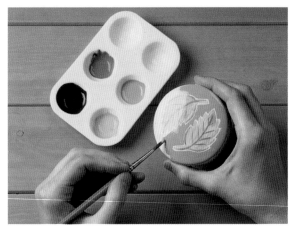

10 Paint the background of the lid, as before. Leave the paint to dry. Paint the remaining jars in complementary colours.

Above: Paint a set of jars in contrasting colours for a cheerful shelf display.

CITRUS FRUIT BOWL

These stencilled limes look terrific adorning a fruit bowl, but they would look just as good on other types of bowl if you wished.

YOU WILL NEED
soft pencil
tracing paper
stencil card (cardboard)
masking tape
craft knife or scalpel
self-healing cutting mat
plain fruit bowl
cleaning fluid
cloth
yellow chinagraph pencil
water-based ceramic paints: citrus green,
mid green, dark green and yellow
artist's paintbrushes
paint palette
acrylic varnish, optional

1 Draw a freehand lime on to tracing paper and transfer it to stencil card (cardboard).

2 Cut out the lime stencil using a sharp craft knife or scalpel and a self-healing cutting mat.

3 Clean the bowl. Attach the stencil to the bowl using masking tape. Draw inside the stencil outline on to the bowl using a yellow chinagraph pencil. Repeat to draw several limes all over the bowl.

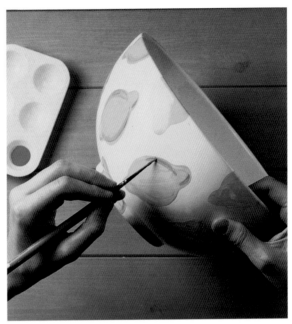

4 Fill in the limes with citrus green paint. Let the paint dry.

5 Add mid green highlights to the fruits and allow the paint to dry.

6 Paint a stalk at the end of each lime in dark green. Let the paint dry.

7 Paint the background, all over the bowl, yellow, leaving a thin white outline around each lime.

8 Paint on varnish or bake the bowl in the oven, following the paint manufacturer's instructions.

MATERIALS

MASKING FLUID

Watercolour art masking fluid is used to mask off areas of the design while colour is applied to the surrounding area. Apply to a clean dry surface. Always allow the masking fluid to dry before painting.

PAINTS

The range of paints available is diverse and the only definitive guide to follow is the manufacturer's instruction on the particular product you buy. All the paints used in this book can be dried or hardened in a domestic oven. If the object is likely to come into contact with food or drink the paint must first be fired in a pottery kiln. Any paints which are not fired in a pottery kiln will not be foodsafe. If the item is not fired, the only way to ensure it is foodsafe is to design it in such a way that the area coming into contact with either the food, liquid or mouth is not painted. Non-foodsafe items should be used for decorative purposes only: remember to mark pieces as such if you give them away as presents.

Enamel Paints

These paints are not made exclusively for china and ceramics. They are available in a range of colours and they dry to an extremely hard durable finish. These paints contain lead and should only ever be used for decorative purposes.

Solvent-based Ceramic Paints

These come in a huge range of colours and lend themselves well to varied painting styles such as wash effects. White spirit can be used to dilute the paint and to clean brushes after use. Solvent-based paints take approximately 24 hours to dry. They can be varnished to protect the finish.

Water-based Ceramic Paints

Sold under various trade names and specially made for painting glazed ceramics, these paints are available in a range of colours. They produce a strong, opaque, flat colour and can be diluted with water. Wash brushes in warm water immediately after painting. Water-based paints dry in around three hours; do not attempt to bake them until they are completely dry or the colour may bubble. Baking the painted item will make the colour durable enough to wash in a dishwasher. Place the item in a cold oven and after baking do not remove it until it has completely cooled. Follow the paint manufacturer's instructions for the temperature and baking times. It is a good idea to do a test first as over-firing can turn the colour slightly brown.

Quick-drying water-based ceramic paints (right) were created specifically for use on china and ceramics. Used with masking fluid (bottom right), these paints offer endless possibilities for painted china designs.

EQUIPMENT

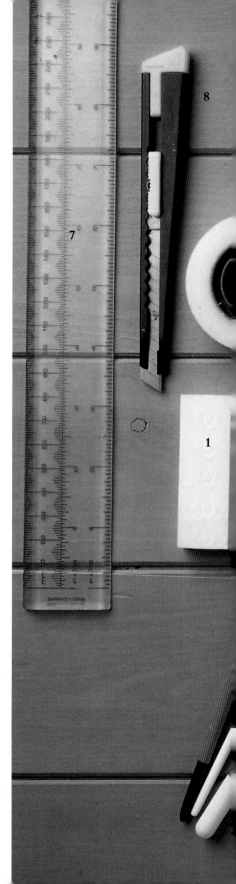

ERASER (1)
As well as being used to remove pencil marks from paper, pencil erasers are used in this book as printing blocks. The design is easily cut into the eraser, using a scalpel or craft knife.

LOW-TACK ADHESIVE TAPE (2)
Use to hold templates or stencils in place on the china if masking tape is not available.

MASKING TAPE (3)
This is useful for holding stencils in place and can be removed easily without damaging the painted surface. Use to mask off areas of the item when painting straight lines.

PAINTBRUSHES (4)
Choose sable watercolour paintbrushes in a range of sizes, including a fine brush for painting lines and details, and a broad soft brush for covering larger areas. Good synthetic brushes are adequate and affordable. It is essential to clean brushes carefully and thoroughly after use. Brushes should never be left standing in pots of water as this will damage the bristles.

PAINT PALETTES (5)
A paint palette is very useful for mixing the colour and texture of paint required, and also allows you to control how much paint you use when sponging. Remember to mix enough colour for the whole project at the beginning; trying to remix a matching colour halfway through painting is almost impossible.

PENCILS AND PENS (6)
A hard lead pencil such as a 2H is good for transferring designs with carbon paper. For marking the ceramic surface directly, a softer 2B lead or chinagraph pencil or a fine felt-tipped pen would be more suitable.

RULER (7)
A good quality metal or plastic ruler makes measuring and cutting easier and more accurate. Wooden rulers have less accurate markings and are liable to be cut accidentally.

SCALPEL OR CRAFT KNIFE (8)
Scalpels with disposable blades are the most accurate cutting tools, especially for cutting stencils. Craft knives are a good alternative, and those with economical break-off blades mean you will always have a very sharp blade.

SCISSORS (9)
Use scissors to cut larger shapes and curves, or when several layers of paper are to be cut together.

SPONGES (10)
Use to produce interesting effects for anything from an even to a textured finish. Both natural and synthetic sponges can be used.

BASIC TECHNIQUES

The projects in this book do not require any specialist skills but it is worth
practising a few painting techniques before you start. The tips and techniques
suggested below will prove useful as you work through the projects.

CLEANING CHINA

Before painting any white china, always clean it
thoroughly to remove any invisible traces of dirt or
grease. Effective cleaning agents are cleaning fluid,
turpentine, methylated spirit (denatured alcohol),
white spirit or lighter fuel. Make sure there are no
naked flames around when using these materials.

SAFE DRINKING VESSELS

To ensure that there is no possibility of any paint
being swallowed when drinking from a mug or glass,
adapt designs so that any colour you paint is at least
3 cm/1¼ in below the rim of drinking vessels.
Otherwise the piece should be fired in a kiln.

PREPARING A SPONGE

Use a scalpel or craft knife to cut cubes of sponge for
sponging paint. Holding the sponge taut as you slice
down into the sponge will make cutting easy and the
lines straight. Keep several cubes to hand when sponging as you may need to change them often.

TESTING A SPONGE

Before sponging on to your china after loading the sponge with paint, test the print on a scrap piece of paper. The first print or two will be too saturated with paint to achieve a pleasing effect.

PRINTING BLOCKS

As with sponging, test the print on scrap paper before you print on the china. When using printing blocks, roll the block lightly on to the surface to ensure you get a good even print.

REMOVING MASKING TAPE OR FILM

When using masking tape or film, it is better to remove it before the paint is completely dry as this will give a cleaner edge to the pattern beneath.

USING PAINTBRUSHES

Always use an appropriately sized paintbrush for the task in hand. Larger areas should always be painted with a large brush using bold strokes, while small, fine brushes are best for detailed work.

TESTING NEW TECHNIQUES

Always test out a technique that you have not tried before. Apply the new technique to a spare piece of china, which can be cleaned up easily, rather than a piece you are already in the process of decorating.

SPONGING VARIATIONS

A stencilled design can be made more interesting by varying the density of the sponging within the image or by adding more than one colour. Allowing the first coat of paint to dry partially before the application of the second will mean that there is more contrast and less blending of the two colours.

WHITE LINES

If you want to leave thin lines of china showing through areas of colour, paint them in first with masking fluid. This can be gently peeled off when the paint is dry to reveal the white china beneath. Use a sharp-pointed instrument such as a craft knife or compass point to lift off the dried masking fluid.

PAINTS

Paints suitable for applying to china are available in water or oil-based types. When mixing up a shade of your own, remember that the two types of paint cannot be intermixed.

WATERY EFFECTS

You can achieve a watery effect in oil-based colours by diluting paints with white spirit. Water-based paints are diluted by adding water.

TRACING

Use tracing paper and a soft pencil to transfer designs directly on to the surface of china. First trace the template or the design you wish to use, then fix the tracing paper to the china with masking tape. Gently rub over the traced design with a soft pencil to transfer.

STRAIGHT LINES

Masking tape is useful for painting straight edges, stripes and even checks and squares. Just stick it down to mark out areas you do not want painted and apply the paint. Remove the tape before the paint is completely dry; straight lines of paint will be left.

REMOVING UNWANTED PAINT

Use a pencil eraser or cotton buds (swabs) to tidy up
a design or to wipe off small areas of unwanted paint.
For larger areas use a damp paper towel or cloth.
Allow the cleaned area to dry before repainting.

REMOVING GUIDE MARKINGS

Pencil or pen guide marks on the china can be easily
wiped off once the paint is completely dry or has
been baked. Use a damp paper towel or cloth and
take care not to rub the paint too hard.

USING MASKING FLUID

Add a drop of water-based paint to masking fluid
before use when working on china that is completely
white. This will help you to see where the masking
fluid has been applied, enabling you to wipe it off
easily when you are ready to do so.

PREPARING A STENCIL

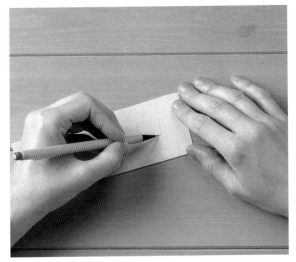

1 Draw a freehand shape or trace and transfer a template from the back of the book on to a piece of stencil card (cardboard).

2 Using a craft knife or scalpel, metal ruler and self-healing cutting mat, cut away the shape, leaving the card border intact.

3 Attach the stencil to the china piece with masking tape. Paint or sponge print over the stencil, taking care not to go over the outside edge of the card. Leave the paint to dry completely.

4 To transfer a detailed design using carbon paper, place the stencil over a piece of carbon paper, carbon side down. Very gently, draw the outline of your design through the stencil hole onto the carbon paper, using a fine felt-tipped pen. Attach the carbon paper to the china piece with masking tape. Use a soft pencil to lightly trace the shape on to the china.

TEMPLATES

Enlarge the templates on a photocopier, or trace the design and draw a grid of squares over your tracing. Draw a larger grid on another piece of paper and copy the outline square by square.

Seashore Bathroom Set, pp. 33–35

Vegetable Storage Jars, pp. 40–42

Bedroom Lampbase, pp. 43–45

Summer Tea Service, pp. 46–49

Child's Teaset, pp. 50–53

SUPPLIERS

UNITED KINGDOM
Alec Tiranti
70 High Street
Theale
Reading RG7 5AR
Tel: (01734) 302775

Atlantis Art Materials
146 Brick Lane
London EC1 6RU
Tel: (0171) 3778855

Edgar Udney & Co. Ltd
314 Balham High Road
London SW17
Tel: (0181) 7678181

London Graphic Centre
16 Shelton Street
London WC2
Tel: (0171) 2400095

Panduro Hobby
Westward House
Transport Avenue
Brentford
Middlesex TW8 9HF
Tel: (01392) 427788

UNITED STATES
The Art Store
935 Erie Blvd. E.
Syracuse, NY 13210

Art Essentials of New York Ltd
3 Cross Street
Suffern
NY 10901
Tel: (800) 283 5323

Createx Colors
14 Airport Park Road
East Granby
CT 06026
Tel: (860) 653 5505

Dick Blick
P.O. Box 1267
Galesburg
IL 61402
Tel: (309) 343 6181

Hofcraft
P.O. Box 72
Grand Haven
MI 49417
Tel: (800) 828 0359

CANADA
Abby Arts & Crafts
4118 Hastings Street
Burnaby, BC
Tel: (604) 299 5201

Lewis Craft
2300 Younge Street
Toronto, Ont
Tel: (416) 483 2783

AUSTRALIA
Spotlight (60 stores)
Tel: (freecall) 1800 500021

Lincraft
(stores in every capital)
Tel: (03) 9875 7575

ACKNOWLEDGEMENTS

The publishers would like to thank the following people: Karen Craggs for the Starburst Bathroom Tiles and Pasta Bowls; Ken Eardley for the Espresso Cups and Saucers and Checkerboard Dinner Plate; Mary Fellows for the Snowflake Plate, Hand-painted Mugs, Mosaic Flowerpot and Saucer, Carnival Vase, Autumn Leaf Coffee Pot and Funky Condiment Set; Helen Musselwhite for the Seashore Bathroom Set, Vegetable Storage Jars, Bedroom Lampbase, Summer Tea Service and Child's Teaset; Marie Perkins for the Sunflower Vase, Kitchen Herb Jars and Citrus Fruit Bowl; Isabel Stanley for the 1950s Jug and Butter Dish and Abstract Egg Cups.

INDEX